D0710731

Wyoming
The Equality State

Marcia Amidon Lusted

PowerKiDS press.

New York

For Mom and Dad and their years in Newcastle, Wyoming

Published in 2011 by The Rosen Publishing Group, Inc.
29 East 21st Street, New York, NY 10010

First Edition

Editor: Maggie Murphy
Book Design: Greg Tucker
Photo Researcher: Jessica Gerweck

Photo Credits: Cover, pp. 5, 9, 11, 15, 19, 22 (tree, animal, flag, flower) Shutterstock.com; p. 7 John Hauser/Getty Images; p. 13 Darrell Gulin/Getty Images; p. 17 Macduff Everton/Getty Images; p. 22 (bird) © www.iStockphoto.com/Steve Byland; p. 22 (Penny Wolin) © Penny Wolin; p. 22 (Patricia Maclachlan) by John MacLachlan, provided by HarperCollins Publishers; p. 22 (Jackson Pollock) Tony Vaccaro/Getty Images.

Library of Congress Cataloging-in-Publication Data

Lusted, Marcia Amidon.
  Wyoming : the Equality State / Marcia Amidon Lusted. — 1st ed.
     p. cm. — (Our amazing states)
  Includes index.
  ISBN 978-1-4488-0663-8 (library binding) — ISBN 978-1-4488-0762-8 (pbk.) — ISBN 978-1-4488-0763-5 (6-pack)
  1. Wyoming—Juvenile literature. I. Title.
  F761.3.L87 2011
  978.7—dc22
                                    2009053087

Manufactured in the United States of America

CPSIA Compliance Information: Batch #WS10PK: For Further Information contact Rosen Publishing, New York, New York at 1-800-237-9932

Contents

Cowboys and Dinosaur Bones

There is a state where cowboys and cowgirls still take part in roping and riding events. Dinosaur bones are found in **fossil** beds. The nation's first national **monument**, Devils Tower, rises above the plains. Where are we? We are in Wyoming!

Wyoming is in the western part of the United States. It is located between Idaho and South Dakota. It is north of Colorado and south of Montana. The U.S. government owns almost half of the land in Wyoming.

Wyoming is nicknamed the Equality State because it was the first state to allow women the right to vote, serve on juries, and hold public office. Wyoming gave women equality with men before any other state did.

The Teton Range, shown here, is one of Wyoming's many mountain ranges. In front of the mountains, the Snake River curves at a place called Oxbow Bend.

Native Americans and Pioneers

The first people to live in Wyoming were Native Americans such as the Shoshones, the Sioux, and the Cheyennes. Around 1807, John Colter became the first white man to travel through Wyoming and see its **geysers** and hot springs. He was a member of the Lewis and Clark expedition, which was sent to travel through the West after the **Louisiana Purchase** in 1803.

Later **pioneers** passed through Wyoming on the Oregon Trail, a wagon trail leading from Missouri to Oregon. Cowboys worked for huge cattle ranches. Soon the Union Pacific Railroad was built, linking the eastern and western United States. Part of it passed through Wyoming. In 1890, Wyoming became the forty-fourth state.

Here, a painting from 1896 shows Native Americans carrying guns while riding on horseback near Cheyenne, Wyoming.

Wyoming has both the high tops of the Rocky Mountains and the grassy open spaces of the Great Plains. In between is the Wyoming Basin, which has dry deserts and sand dunes. Wyoming also has many rivers, such as the Yellowstone, Bighorn, and Snake. Some of these rivers have cut deep **canyons** into the land. The Yellowstone River has two huge waterfalls.

Wyoming has one of the driest **climates** in the United States. Summers are short and hot while winters are very cold. Most parts of Wyoming get very little rain during the year. However, it can snow as much as 200 inches (508 cm) throughout the year in the mountains! Wyoming is also very windy.

The tops of the mountains in the Teton Range, in northwest Wyoming, are covered with snow throughout most of the year.

Herds of bighorn sheep live in Wyoming's mountains. Elks, antelope, and prairie dogs live on the plains and in the deserts. Rattlesnakes crawl among the rocks and grasses. Wild horses run free in the Pryor Mountain Wild Horse Range. Golden eagles, trumpeter swans, and great blue herons fly through Wyoming's skies. Grizzly bears wander through Yellowstone Park, along with herds of bison.

Wyoming has more kinds of grass than kinds of trees, but ponderosa pines are found in the Black Hills and cottonwoods grow near streams. The state flower, Indian paintbrush, is a bright red flower that grows on the prairies. Sagebrush and wheatgrass grow in the basin area.

Here, two male bighorn sheep ram their horns together. Bighorn sheep live in Wyoming's mountains where they are safe from predators, such as coyotes.

What Do People Do in Wyoming?

Many people in Wyoming work in mining and at oil wells in the plains. Petroleum, gas, and coal are also produced there. Uranium, which is used in power plants to make electricity, also comes from Wyoming's mines. Wood from Wyoming's forests is cut down and sold.

Wyoming also has many farmers. Sugar beets, hay, and wheat are grown there, and cattle and sheep feed on the plains' grasses. Ranch owners still use cowboys to tend their herds of cattle.

Visitors come to Wyoming to see its scenery. Many people work in the hotels and restaurants where these visitors stay and eat, especially near Yellowstone National Park. Many movies and television shows are also made in Wyoming.

In Wyoming, you can both see wild horses and ride on horseback at a ranch. This cowboy is rounding up horses on a ranch near Shell Valley, Wyoming.

A Frontier Town and a State Capital

Cheyenne started as a Wild West **frontier** town for railroad workers and soldiers. Once the railroad was finished, though, the town grew larger and became a center for entertainment and a place where people could hear news from the East. When Wyoming became a state, Cheyenne became its capital.

Cheyenne has many places where visitors can learn about its frontier history, such as the Frontier Days Old West Museum and the Wyoming State Museum. Cheyenne holds Frontier Days every year, when cowboys and cowgirls take part in rodeos. You can also visit the University of Wyoming Archaeological Dig Site nearby and see Indian relics and prehistoric **artifacts**. You could also visit a bison ranch and try herding bison on horseback!

Here, young Native American girls dance at Cheyenne's Frontier Days. Frontier Days have been held in Cheyenne every year since 1897.

A Trip Through Time

About 50 million years ago, during the **Cenozoic era**, three ancient lakes existed in southwest Wyoming. When they dried up, they left behind the fossils of many different plants and animals. In 1972, this area, called the Green River Formation, became Fossil Butte National Monument.

Some of the best-**preserved** fossils in the world are found here. Fossilized fish, insects, plants, reptiles, birds, and mammals are all amazingly preserved. These fossils include ancient stingrays, crocodiles, turtles, bats, and dog-sized horses. The Green River Formation fossils are the best **paleontological** record of plants and animals living near water in North America during the Tertiary, or third, period of the Cenozoic era.

These are fossils of Priscacara fish found in the Green River Formation, at the Fossil Butte National Monument.

Hot Springs and Gushing Geysers

One of Wyoming's most famous places is Yellowstone National Park. Yellowstone was America's first national park, created in 1872. Most of the park is in Wyoming, although parts of it are in Montana and Idaho.

The park has many different types of wildlife for visitors to see, such as grizzly bears, moose, elks, bison, and wolves. However, Yellowstone is best known for its geothermal features, which were created by heat from inside Earth. The area itself was once a **volcano**. More than 300 geysers, such as Old Faithful, shoot hot water into the air. Mud pots and fumaroles, or steam vents, bubble and hiss. Hot springs in beautiful colors are found throughout the park.

Old Faithful, one of Yellowstone's famous geysers, is shown erupting here. *Inset*: A bison walks around the Emerald Pool in the park's Black Sand Basin.

Come to Wyoming!

Whether you like Wild West history or studying rock formations, Wyoming has something for you. At the Buffalo Bill Historical Center, you can learn about one of Wyoming's most famous people and his Wild West show. You can also visit the Devils Tower National Monument, a huge tower of rock that rises more than 1,200 feet (370 m) from the ground. It was once the center of an ancient volcano.

Would you like to see the names of some of the pioneers who traveled through Wyoming? If you would, then visit Independence Rock, where thousands of them cut their names and the dates they were there into a rock cliff. No matter what you like to do, Wyoming is a beautiful and interesting place to live or visit!

artifacts (AR-tih-fakts) Objects created and produced by humans.

canyons (KAN-yunz) Deep, narrow valleys.

Cenozoic era (seh-neh-ZOH-ik ER-uh) A time period over 65 million years ago.

climates (KLY-mits) The kind of weather certain places have.

fossil (FO-sul) The hardened remains of a dead animal or plant.

frontier (frun-TEER) The edge of a settled country, where the wilderness begins.

geysers (GY-zerz) Springs that send up jets of hot water or steam.

Louisiana Purchase (loo-ee-zee-AN-uh PUR-chus) Land that the United States bought from France in 1803.

monument (MON-yuh-mint) An honored place.

paleontological (pay-lee-on-tuh-LO-jih-kul) Having to do with the study of things that lived in the past.

pioneers (py-uh-NEERZ) Some of the first people to settle in a new area.

preserved (prih-ZURVD) To have been kept whole or almost whole.

volcano (vol-KAY-noh) An opening in the surface of Earth that sometimes shoots up a hot liquid rock called lava.

Wyoming State Symbols

State Tree
Cottonwood

State Animal
Bison

State Flag

State Bird
Western
Meadowlark

State Flower
Indian
Paintbrush

State Seal

Famous People from Wyoming

Jackson Pollock
(1912–1956)
Born in Cody, WY
Artist

Patricia MacLachlan
(1938–)
Born in Cheyenne, WY
Author

Penny Wolin
(1953–)
Born in Cheyenne, WY
Photographer

Wyoming State Map

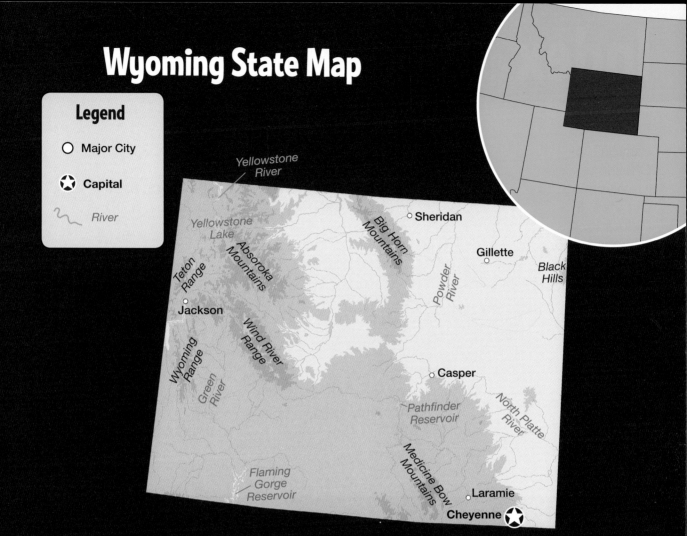

Legend

○ Major City

⭐ Capital

〰 River

Wyoming State Facts

Population: About 493,782

Area: 97,818 square miles (253,344 sq km)

Motto: "Equal Rights"

Song: "Wyoming," words by C. E. Winter and music by G. E. Knapp

Index

Web Sites

Due to the changing nature of Internet links, PowerKids Press has developed an online list of Web sites related to the subject of this book. This site is updated regularly. Please use this link to access the list:

www.powerkidslinks.com/amst/wy/

24